GU____

free

MUM

GUILT-FREE MUM

An Hachette UK Company
www.hachette.co.uk

Vie Books, an imprint of Summersdale Publishers Ltd
Part of Octopus Publishing Group Limited
Carmelite House
50 Victoria Embankment
LONDON
EC4Y 0DZ
UK

www.summersdale.com

Printed and bound in Poland

ISBN: 978-1-80007-937-3

Substantial discounts on bulk quantities of Summersdale books are available to corporations, professional associations and other organizations. For details contact general enquiries: telephone: +44 (0) 1243 771107 or email: enquiries@summersdale.com.

GUILT-free MUM

HOW TO BE KIND TO YOUR MIND

ZEENA MOOLLA

DISCLAIMER

The information given in this book should not be treated as a substitute for qualified medical advice. Neither the author nor the publisher can be held responsible for any loss or claim arising out of the use, or misuse, of the suggestions made or the failure to take medical advice. The case studies and quotes included in this book are based on the real experiences of individuals and families, however, in some cases, names have been changed to protect privacy. Although there is a move toward more gender-neutral language, for the purposes of this book, the term breastfeeding is used throughout.

CONTENTS

INTRODUCTION

It's fair to say that motherhood and guilt are intertwined. According to numerous studies, many mums, particularly new mothers, experience feelings of guilt, leaving them with an overwhelming sense of failure. This is unsurprising given that many of us live in societies where the expected level of parental engagement is enormous. Vast shelves of books, targeted largely at mums, are dogmatically devoted to concepts of how to parent a child.

One particular piece of parental research discovered mothers are more likely than fathers to view taking a nap as self-care (64 per cent versus 47 per cent) and mums are also more prone to feeling overwhelmed and burnt out (66 per cent versus 53 per cent). When you consider the same study found mothers more likely to express guilt at the very notion of self-care, it's apparent that mum guilt has the potential to be very detrimental to a mother's physical and mental well-being.

This is book is designed to walk you through identifying, tackling and overcoming mum guilt, particularly in the first stages of motherhood, because when shame is overshadowing your experience of becoming a mum, it needs dealing with. Being a mum will undoubtedly have its challenges, but guilt shouldn't rob you of any joyous moments you deserve with your beautiful baby. Now *that* would be the real shame.

THE MANY GUISES OF MUM GUILT

Guilt is a powerful emotion. It can encourage you to have accountability for your actions and fuel motivation to improve your behaviour. Often, however, and particularly in motherhood, guilt can distort into unnecessary fixation and detrimental habits – sometimes, in ways you're not even aware of. This chapter explores the many guises of guilt and how it manifests in motherhood. In order to overcome it, you need to recognize it.

I sometimes think that they take the baby out and they put the guilt in.

♥ ARIANNA HUFFINGTON

NEGATIVE SELF-TALK

"I'm a terrible mother."
"That mum is a natural at motherhood – I wish I was."
"I'm failing my child."

The above are typical examples of negative thoughts a mum might have in early motherhood. In a study carried out in the UK and Ireland of 395 new mothers with babies under one, nearly two-thirds admitted to having repetitive thoughts about being a "bad mother". As the study demonstrates, thoughts like these are very common and often symptomatic of overwhelming feelings of guilt and worry. If you find your train of thought creeping towards negative self-talk, remind yourself that you're far from alone in experiencing such inner dialogue. Most importantly, these thoughts are only reflective of unfounded fears, *not* your abilities as a mother.

ANXIETY

Anxiety is a perfectly natural emotion, particularly in early motherhood. It is often an instinctive reaction to a situation to keep both you and your baby safe. For instance, your baby's low immunity and a nasty bug doing the rounds could make you anxious enough to avoid the local soft play or busy shopping mall. While your thought process might involve an element of anxiety, behind that apprehension is some logic and a perfectly reasonable response. However, when anxiety becomes all-consuming to the point of affecting your mental and physical health, your sense of burden and guilt around motherhood needs exploring.

If you're sometimes finding yourself overcome by the guilt evoked by a prospective situation with your baby, perhaps even catastrophizing it, slow down your thoughts and pay attention to what you're thinking.

Ask yourself:

- Am I anxious because the responsibility of motherhood feels overwhelming?
- Does this sort of situation make me excessively worry about being a bad mother?
- Am I overthinking potential worst-case scenarios?
- Am I physically affected by the anxiety?
- Is this sort of anxiety inhibiting my life?

By addressing your feelings in such detail, you will start to notice and recognize where anxiety is becoming an issue. Guilt may well be playing a big part in that. As you grow more familiar with the causes of escalating anxiety, you can challenge your negative thought patterns and look at how you might allay your concern, perhaps through mindful or therapeutic means. Acknowledging what you're feeling and why are crucial first steps.

LOW SELF-WORTH

It's not unusual for a new mum to still be in pyjamas at lunchtime, dining on scant, unwholesome meals of chocolate, crackers and dips. But when this is typically less about being time-poor and more about a behavioural pattern, it could be indicative of low self-worth. Research carried out in the Netherlands shows that esteem can often plunge in new motherhood, since in navigating unfamiliar territory, feelings of inadequacy and the subsequent guilt this often breeds take their toll. Consequently, things like showering or eating properly, even when the opportunity arises, can take a back seat as mothers feel their needs are not worthy of prioritizing. It's almost a form of self-flagellation and it's an easy-to-overlook guise of mum guilt, especially given that being "maternal" is often conflated with selflessness and martyrdom.

However, if you find yourself regularly denying your own needs without real reason, look at unpicking why that is and, if guilt is festering at the root, confront this. Remind yourself you're a human being simply doing your best in unchartered, often turbulent, circumstances and you have nothing to feel guilty for. And remember your worth because to be the best possible mother you can for your baby, you have to take care of your needs, too. Both you and your baby deserve this.

ANGER

Human beings experience a whole range of emotions. When it comes to motherhood, particularly in the early stages, the sheer frustration, fear of failing and resentment of a situation can lead to guilt which in turn can become anger. Here's an important message to be repeated throughout this book: anger does *not* make you a bad mother. Ask any experienced, honest mum if temper has ever been an issue during a particularly challenging parenting moment, and it's likely the answer is yes! So, while losing your temper is not ideal, it's a perfectly comprehensible upshot when your nerves have taken a battering from perhaps a baby on nap strike or a meltdown of excruciating proportions. That said, when it becomes a go-to response or your anger feels more like rage, your emotional reactions need attention. As rage and guilt can become cyclical behaviours, acknowledging this will help you to begin breaking that pattern.

I had a lot of guilt as a single mother trying to raise a child... You have to give yourself permission to let go of the guilt.

———————

SHERRI SHEPHERD

Social Media Overuse

Most new parents want to flood the internet with photos and updates about their new baby. For many new mums, perhaps during a late-night feed or trapped under a chest-hugging napping baby, a scroll through social media provides a means of feeling in touch, and let's be fair, it is a great boredom release. However, for some mothers, excessive social media may be a subconscious expression of guilt. Online, you're able to present an entirely different world to the one you're inhabiting, concealing feelings of inadequacy behind reams of positive posts. A recent study carried out by Ohio State University reported that new mums who posted on social media the most were more likely to feel pressure to be "perfect" mothers.

If this sounds familiar, look at how much time you're spending on social media and why. This isn't intended as a self-berating process for spending too much time on your phone or the internet – it's simply a way to assess if mum guilt is the impetus for any excess use.

ACCEPTING GUILT

Let's be clear here, all loving parents are likely to experience a degree of guilt at some point – it's simply a sign of strong attachment and commitment to a child! And yes, sometimes that guilt might be warranted. Raising a voice at a tantrumming toddler, losing patience over potty training, being overly strict with a teen – these are just a few examples in the rich and varied journey of motherhood where a mum might experience justifiable guilt. However, a healthy relationship with guilt is accepting it as a natural response rather than letting it interfere with your life and behaviour. In order to keep guilt from spiralling, self-compassion is key, so if you know you're not strong on this, vow to make a concerted effort to change that now.

THE
FOURTH
TRIMESTER

The first twelve weeks of motherhood, otherwise known as the "fourth trimester", are brimming with emotions, from elation to frustration and everything in between. Often, one of the biggest sensations a new mum encounters is guilt. It likes to set up nice and early in your brain and if left untackled, enjoys permanent residence long after your child has grown up and left home! During this emotionally vulnerable time, guilt can be such an unhealthy frame of mind for a new mother – so let's start tackling it.

Give yourself
permission
to fail.
The guilt that
we place on
ourselves as
parents is
tremendous.

♥ SHONDA RHIMES

WHERE'S MY MATERNAL INSTINCT?

During the early days of motherhood, you may wonder where your maternal instinct is hiding. Surely this all should come naturally? Instead, you may wish you had a 24-7 nanny or find yourself consulting the myriad baby manuals and online advice for help. Despite such insecurity being hugely common, notions of "maternal instinct" as something innate are so widely touted in society, it can leave many new mums fearful they're somehow failing at motherhood if they don't immediately feel it.

Rest assured, you will undoubtedly develop a gut instinct about your child. Some things will come naturally, while other stuff you'll learn. New motherhood is often fraught with self-doubt – but never take the lack of a fully-formed maternal instinct to mean you don't have a connection to your child. Most importantly, never mistake a perfectly natural lack of confidence as a barometer for the kind of mum you are.

VISITING HOURS
ARE OVER

A new baby is often a source of much excitement. Consequently, while undertaking the small matter of how to raise a tiny human, many mothers find themselves contending with a steady stream of visitors, too. However, if you're not in the mood for guests and are struggling to follow your own train of thought, let alone a conversation about what the traffic was like on the way over, don't do it! When you're the mother of a new baby, being "on form" for everyone shouldn't feel like an obligation, so try to master the art of saying "no". If you can't face it, enlist a partner or relative to act as "baby bouncer". Most importantly, remind yourself that you and your baby are the priority right now and people-pleasing is not something that should be weighing on your conscience at all.

KITCHEN IS CLOSED!

It doesn't matter if your idea of cooking is finding a couple of slices of cheese at the back of the fridge and grilling them on toast; preparing meals shouldn't be the sole responsibility of any mother – especially a new one. If you have a partner, let them make the meals. Welcome visitors on the understanding you won't be providing a cordon bleu meal. If they can bring a curry or casserole to share or stick in your freezer, even better! Embrace takeout menus and simple meals. Cooking, particularly during the first few weeks of motherhood, should never feel like a guilt-driven duty for you to bear in miserable isolation.

Make Peace With Mess

Stop! Step away from that kitchen scourer! Much like cooking, cleaning shouldn't just be a mother's domain and will likely be the furthest thing from your mind during the early weeks of motherhood, when all your capacity is taken up with your new baby. If you can, make peace with your house closely resembling the scene of a burglary for now – there will be time for a tidy home in the near future, but now is not the moment. Make housework the onus of partners, friends, relatives – but *not* you, because this sort of misplaced responsibility should be the furthest thing from a new mum's conscience.

NO SLEEP SHAME

As many new mums discover, the recommendation to try to sleep the minute the baby hits the Moses basket is a popular piece of advice. It's a sensible suggestion of course, but it's easier said than done when this is often the only opportunity you have to shower, eat something or enjoy a whole hot drink without it turning stone cold. So don't let the "sleep while baby sleeps" adage become a source of guilt! Eating, bathing, relaxing with a hot drink, enjoying a new series – these are all vital forms of rejuvenation, too.

NEW-PARENT ROWS

If you're raising your baby with a partner and suddenly find yourselves rowing more frequently, perhaps even turning the air blue with some very choice words, you are far from alone. Research has shown that nine out of ten new parents admit they row more often once a baby enters their lives. The newborn weeks are the most testing of times for a relationship, so go easy on yourselves and don't consider a barbed remark or late-night argument as indicative of the kind of people you are or your relationship's future. You're two new parents trying your best to look after a baby on ridiculously low levels of sleep; things *will* get tetchy on occasion. Dwelling on any shame or remorse is a waste of valuable energy when really, it would be more surprising if you didn't row!

The thing about parenting rules is there aren't any. That's what makes it so difficult.

———————————

EWAN McGREGOR

FEEDING FRENZY

Once your baby has been born, it might feel that how to feed your baby is a matter of everyone's concern, with your perspective and needs vastly and dangerously overlooked. If you're feeling pressured or "spoken over" with regards to how you feed your baby, be it bottle or breast, some boundaries need to be set. Practise holding your nerve by smiling and saying out loud: "*I'll decide what's best for my baby and myself.*" Now believe it! Other people's opinions on matters that don't concern them can become a source of manipulated and coerced guilt you can definitely do without. Remind yourself frequently: in order to be the best possible mother to your baby, *you* matter – and everyone, including yourself, needs to be clear on this.

BOTTLE OR BREAST = BOND

Here's some simple truth for you: the unconditional love you receive from your child is unwavering, and the way you feed them will never change that. No matter what breast-vs-bottle war a newspaper, website or overshared opinion may wage, research carried out in the UK shows that there is no correlation between the bond of a mother and baby and how the baby is fed. If you experience a feeling of shame for whichever way you feed your baby, never lose sight of the fact that even on your most testing days, your mere presence can soothe your baby.

Resenting Motherhood

"Cherish every moment" is a phrase a new mum will hear often, sometimes long before the baby's even out. But let's face it, while you're surviving on 45 minutes of sleep, have sick in your hair and haven't had a chance to dine on much besides a handful of biscuits, it's not always easy advice to follow. So don't! Allow yourself to embrace how you're feeling. Don't feel guilty admitting to the moments in which you're feeling resentful of motherhood. This will never make you a bad mum. It makes you a human being.

Motherhood
is a like a big
sleeping bag
of guilt.

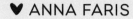 ANNA FARIS

NO WEIGHT WATCHING!

During labour and throughout the early days of looking after their child, a new mum is pushed physically to the max. From taking baby for walks in their pram to rocking them to soothe them, not to mention the energy that's consumed from being up all hours of the day and night, it's a tiring business. And if you breastfeed, this is another calorie-burning activity to add to the list. It's pretty clear that research shows new mothers need extra energy! So now is not the time to feel any guilt around food consumption or weight gain. While eating nutritious foods is important for your vitality, worrying about weight gain could be detrimental to it.

BORN THIS WAY

Some mums give birth with the aid of epidurals. Some have C-sections. Others bring their babies into the world completely drug-free. There are those whose babies enter this life via surrogacy. Some mothers conceive with fertility help. Some adopt. Among the many routes to motherhood, the only emotion you should feel around your journey is complete pride. If you're experiencing any sense of self-reproach or shame around the details of your path, remember, every story is unique and you're no less or more a mother because of how you became one. A baby with a loving mother is a lucky one; simple as that.

SOLO WARRIOR

"Sometimes, I cannot put into the words how much I love her," said British footballer Marcus Rashford of his mum, who raised him and his siblings alone. "The most extraordinary woman I know," described singer Alicia Keys of her single-parent mother. "I don't know how she did it," admitted pop star Christina Aguilera of her mother's solo parenting. The admiration and immense love a child can have for their single-parent mum is often woefully overlooked in society. If you're a mother raising a baby alone, without doubt you need support and recognition – but never pity or societal shame. Yours is a family to celebrate and, rest assured, the bond you have with your child is second-to-none.

When my daughter says,
"I wish I had a baby sister,"
I am stricken with
guilt and panic.
When she says,
"I only want to eat gum!"
or "Wipe my butt!"
I am less affected.

———————————

TINA FEY

BIRTH PLAN BLUES

If you gave birth to your baby, maybe you'd planned on doing so without an epidural. Perhaps you wanted your baby to be born at home. You might have even hoped to welcome your baby into the world with pain relief no stronger than paracetamol, amid a meadow of lilac and frolicking lambs. Whatever your birth plan was, and however outlandish and unfeasible it might have seemed to others, you have every right to grieve any ideas you had to abandon during labour. These were your delivery dreams and it's quite understandable, and common, to feel a bit deflated if they went unfulfilled. However, be wary of letting quite natural disappointment morph into feelings of failure and guilt. Sooner than you think, those delivery details will be forgotten, but most importantly, your beautiful baby is here and that couldn't be further from failure.

Thief of Joy

Theodore Roosevelt once famously said: "Comparison is the thief of joy." When it comes to parenting, this is never truer. Fixating on your baby's development and what they "should" be doing or how you parent is a dangerous game to play when it leads to feelings of inadequacy and guilt. Every child, parent and circumstance is different – frequently remind yourself of this. Also resist engaging in conversations with other parents where the exchange feels like it's taking a competitive turn. How long your child sleeps for, whether you breastfeed or not, baby milestones – these are typical areas where new mums often report feeling like they're failing if they try to match their experiences with others. In such situations, politely change the subject – you'll be doing yourself and your baby a favour.

MIND YOUR OWN!

Perhaps some of the following sound familiar to you:

"If you hold your baby too much you will spoil them."

"A breastfeeding mother should NEVER drink coffee."

"Sleep training is for people who don't like their children."

"Using formula milk is just lazy parenting!"

No matter how well-intended or thinly-veiled it is, an uninvited opinion can drive a new mother to distraction. For many, it can exacerbate feelings of incompetence and shame – and this is reason alone to shut down this sort of unhelpful judgement. Whether it's directed at you or uttered in casual conversation, find a way to suggest that it's perhaps inappropriate for other people, particularly those without medical qualification, to determine what's best for a mother and baby.

"Oh, I'm just
a mum."
Just a mum?
Please!
Being a mum
is everything.

♥ SALLY FIELD

I MISS MY OLD LIFE!

Grab a sticky note and write on it: "I'm allowed to miss my old life." Now stick that note anywhere you'll regularly see it. These words need to be retained. As research testifies, many new mothers express a type of grief for their former baby-free lives and admit to experiencing shame around such emotions. But it's crucial for your well-being to shift your focus from self-reproach to self-acceptance – especially as missing your old life won't always be confined to challenging moments. A perfectly serene bath time or stress-free trip to a baby group could have your mind wandering, wistfully wishing for the freedom of pre-baby life, too. So, don't suppress or deny how you're feeling. Instead, embrace it. Remind yourself you are far from alone in harbouring these feelings. Remember, your old life hasn't gone away – it's just evolving, with so much to look forward to and this all-consuming phase not a true reflection of what's to come.

CRY BABY

"All babies cry" is a well-worn adage that is never helpful for a new mum to hear, especially when a newborn is in the throes of a particularly shrill and inconsolable meltdown. Yes, of course all babies cry, but that doesn't mean you have to assume the role of a maternal martyr and suppress the natural frustration a bout of relentless crying can induce. It's important that you seek support – from perhaps a friend, partner or relative – to share the load when a persistent crying phase gets too much. Of course, if you're at all concerned about excessive crying, be sure to speak to your doctor or maternity team for advice. But equally essential is ensuring that you're not berating yourself with guilt for an entirely reasonable response to a stressful situation.

BABY SPAM

You might have sworn in your child-free days that you'd never be the type of new mother to litter social media with ultrasound scans, baby photos and endless updates on your little one's progress. Perhaps now, with your beautiful baby here, the internet is practically buckling under the weight of your baby-related posts? If posting about your newborn brings you joy, spam away. Don't feel guilty for "oversharing" or "attention-seeking" or whatever other accusation you might have heard levelled at baby spam – you're simply a proud new parent. How often do you see a social media share of an inspirational quote prefaced with: "Sorry for the mawkish meme spam"? Bear in mind that the overuse of social media could be a sign that you are suffering from parental guilt, but if you don't feel this applies to you and you just want to spread the love, post to your heart's content, and without apology!

I had all this horrible,
self-imposed guilt.
I thought what a
terrible mother I was
for leaving my child
even for like a day.

———————————

GISELE BÜNDCHEN

Separation Anxiety

You might have heard of the term "separation anxiety" in relation to how babies react to being separated from a parent. But often overlooked is the angst a new mum goes through being away from her baby. It might be necessity, such as work or an appointment, but the guilt can be quite overwhelming for lots of mothers, especially during these first few weeks. If you have little choice, it can be tough, but remind yourself that this is unavoidable and with all the right support in place, both you and the baby will be fine. Similarly, if you're away from your baby because it's a break you need, this is necessary, and again, tell yourself this. You need to thrive just like your baby does, so you have to allow yourself space to recharge. This is what both you and your baby deserve.

AGE CONCERN

Newsflash: a baby isn't aware of, and therefore doesn't care about, the age of its mother! The average age of childbirth has been rising steadily since the mid-1960s, and in some countries, more women are happily and healthily giving birth between the ages of 35 and 39. Yet still, many "more mature" mums are made to feel like there's something controversial about their relationship to motherhood. Likewise, a younger-than-average mum can experience similar stigmatizing, guilt-goading attitudes, being conversely deemed not "mature" enough for motherhood. So, here's another newsflash for you: all that matters to a baby is having a nurturing physical and emotional presence! If this is the love your baby is receiving, your age as a mother is irrelevant.

THE MANY FACES OF PND

When actress Gwyneth Paltrow talked openly about her experience with postnatal depression (PND), or postpartum depression (PPD), she articulated brilliantly how symptoms are often not as characteristic as some might think. "I thought postpartum depression meant you were sobbing every single day and incapable of looking after a child. But there are different shades of it and depths of it, which is why I think it's so important for women to talk about it." This is very welcome insight and advice. For many, PND goes undetected thanks to its many guises. Also, PND is not exclusively a hormone-related experience encountered by just birth mothers. No matter your journey to motherhood, often the root causes of PND include that minxy little emotion "mum guilt". If you're experiencing a low mood since becoming a mother, whatever the extent of it, don't trivialize how you're feeling. Talk to a friend or relative, or source professional support. Remember, you don't have to cope alone.

Working mums and stay-at-home mums get a tough time... You just have to do what's right for you and not listen to what the "mummy brigade" say.

♥ HOLLY WILLOUGHBY

CASE STUDY

Be Kind to Yourself

When I announced at work that I was pregnant, I was full of hope that I'd be nipping back to the office soon after the baby was out to visit the women I loved working with. They had all been so excited for me, joyfully revelling in the minutiae of my pregnancy week after week. Lots of them mums themselves, they accompanied me on lunch hours to help pick out and coo over baby paraphernalia, enjoyed endless conversations about preferred names and kindly and quietly took on more of my work as my due date neared. They were utterly amazing.

Of course, when I gave birth, my world changed overnight. With life now so chaotic and the familiar train ride feeling like an impossible feat with a cumbersome pram and leaky boobs, I realized that a lunchtime visit was about as likely as a good night's sleep. I was not only sad at this loss of intense colleague-friendship, but felt an acute sense of guilt, too. I hadn't accounted for feeling like this at all. These women had my back and I couldn't express my gratitude with an introduction to the baby they'd been so invested in while she was in my belly. I felt such an extraordinary sense of shame.

When I finally made it to the office, they were characteristically lovely – and of course, hadn't been tapping their watches wondering why I hadn't shown up with my daughter sooner. They totally got it! In fact, I don't think they'd have held it against me if I hadn't made it in at all throughout my maternity leave. Most people understand the first year of a baby's life is full-on, and just having this sort of understanding and empathy really helped me to stop pressuring myself.

NIKKI, MOTHER OF TWO

THERE'S NO SUCH THING AS THE PERFECT MUM

Motherhood can feel loaded with sanctimonious pressure as notions of what makes a "perfect mum" perpetuates in various forms. From family and friends to the media, a mother might often sense being a mum is dictated by a form of maternal moral code. This chapter explores some of those "commandment-style" ideas around motherhood, from a baby's birth and beyond – and with each, reasons why you need to ditch that guilt!

No one's really doing it perfectly. I think you love your kids with your whole heart, and you do the best you possibly can.

———

REESE WITHERSPOON

THOU SHALT
FOLLOW A ROUTINE

7 a.m.: Gently rouse baby from a blissful 12-hour sleep

7.15 a.m.: Change and dress baby for the day

7.30 a.m.: Make yourself comfortable and give baby the morning feed

8.30 a.m.: Now is the time for an hour's play

9.30 a.m.: As soon as baby looks drowsy, place baby in Moses basket for a 45-minute nap

9.31 a.m.: If by now you are sitting down with a hot drink and a book as your baby blissfully sleeps, then you are very lucky. If instead you are pacing the floor, your hair in a mess, with a cranky baby who does not want a nap at precisely 9.30 a.m., do not fear, you are not alone.

Ditch the Guilt!

Some babies naturally follow a routine. If they do, this is great. If you are not that rare fortunate parent, don't let the pressure of forming a routine become a barometer by which to measure your success. You and your baby will find your own pattern and it's one likely to be dictated by your baby. It may well match a routine you find in a book or online, but often, it will not.

THOU SHALT SWERVE "JUNK" FOOD

Maybe pre-baby you had visions of whipping up batches of organic, wholesome, fresher-than-air meals for your child? Perhaps you shuddered at the mere notion of a jar of pureed fish pie? Possibly, with barely enough time to make a cup of coffee, these visions seem a little ambitious now. Most mums will tell you about how their sanity has been salvaged by the contents of a jar made in a factory and purchased in a frantic hurry from the supermarket – and there should be no shame in that whatsoever!

DITCH THE GUILT!

Change your vernacular around this sort of food. Lose words like "naughty" and "bad" for those days when a pouch of pre-made food has come to the rescue. Instead, adopt terminology more like "easy", "convenient" and "treat". Of course, a nutritious diet for everyone in your family is important to adhere to when possible, but if it isn't, there's nothing healthy about a stressed-out mum.

There is no
such thing as a
perfect parent.
So just be a
real one.

♥ SUE ATKINS

THOU SHALT BAN SCREENS

There's no denying that screens are well and truly ensconced into much family life. An iPad can provide a great distraction for a howling toddler in a restaurant. As your children get older, a laptop is often a homework necessity, while a smartphone can give an anxious parent peace of mind with their teenager. But of course, there's no denying that too much screen time can also prove detrimental. Research has shown excessive exposure to screens can impact negatively on sleep, mood and even physical health thanks to the more sedentary lifestyle it often instigates. However, let's not lose sight of the word "excessive"...

DITCH THE GUILT!

Screen time is a modern parenting conundrum, especially as digitally native children grow alongside rapidly evolving technology. But allowing a child screen time doesn't make a parent less engaged or more negligent. It's a matter of what you consider suitable for your child – and this is for you, and no one else, to decide.

THOU SHALT
NEVER SHOUT

Before you became a mum, you might have witnessed the familiar scene of a mother in a supermarket, clearly out of patience, yelling at a toddler who is lying on the floor, thrashing and screaming like a fish out of water. Maybe the scene had you scuttling off to the safety of the world foods aisle, reassuring yourself you'd never be *that* mother? Well, actually that mother might easily be you. Why? Because, just like that tired, overwrought, frustrated toddler, that yelling mother in the supermarket is equally tired, overwrought and frustrated.

Ditch the Guilt!

Of course, shouting is not the ideal response – there are no winners when both mother and child are in meltdown mode. However, losing your temper on occasion does not make you a terrible parent! In fact, the perfectly natural feeling of guilt that ensues from this sort of scenario pretty much confirms this. What's important though, is that you don't suffocate yourself with that guilt. You can explain to your child, in terms they understand, that shouting is not good conflict resolution and apologize for your own yelling. By showing your capacity to apologize, you are encouraging your child to do the same when they need to. It's crucial you forgive yourself and move on, because dwelling on a perfectly understandable response to a stressful situation is a waste of precious energy.

THOU SHALT SET
A GOOD EXAMPLE

If you look to the internet for the definition of what constitutes setting a "good example" for a child, you will see lists of positive aspects of behaviour such as living in a harmonious environment, never arguing with anyone and always making healthy food choices. Losing patience, bickering with partners and eating unhealthily are deemed as setting a "bad example". But isn't real life made up of all these types of behaviours, both positive and negative? Do you really have to be such a paragon of virtue to be deemed a "good" parent?

Ditch the Guilt!

Firstly, step away from the internet! Secondly, let's change that definition of "good example". Think of a "good example" as an honest, human one. For instance, if you're stuck in stationary traffic for quite some time and begin to lose your patience, you're simply expressing, rather than suppressing, a natural emotion to a frustrating situation. This is a great example of emotional intelligence, particularly when you address specifically how you're feeling to your child. If your child doesn't ever witness you having such emotions, they will come to regard them as "bad" and shameful in themselves. While it's important to manage the intensity of big emotions of course, it's imperative to give both yourself and your child the permission to be human.

Motherhood
should be praised...
But for cultivating
a sense of invisibility,
martyrdom and
tirelessly working
unnoticed and unsung?
Those are not reasons.

———————

SHONDA RHIMES

THOU SHALT ALWAYS LISTEN

There are few things sweeter than a young child desperate to tell a parent about their exciting morning at nursery on the way home. Perhaps there was a dog that ran into the playground, but then Jack cried because he'd forgotten his snack and then later, Anisa did her first ever roly-poly... Between this stream of consciousness and hunting for the after-nursery drink, juggling paintings and bags and navigating the journey home, you might have lost the thread somewhere between the dog and Jack's snack.

Ditch the Guilt!

It can be hard not to feel remorseful when you've zoned out from your child enthusiastically sharing the morning's events with you. But remember to be fair on yourself! Sometimes it will be simply impossible to listen to and retain ALL the information. Of course, you can confess to your child that you lost concentration. After all, they do the same sometimes. Do remember to reassure your child that you will want to hear more when you get home, perhaps over lunch. They may well enjoy telling you all over again! Because who wouldn't want to know what happened to the dog and find out if Jack ever got his snack?

I don't know what I'm doing, but then I have to remind myself no parent does, right?

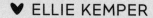 ELLIE KEMPER

THOU SHALT
BE OUTDOORSY

In many nurseries, there is a toy – perhaps a teddy bear or stuffed animal – which is sent home every weekend with a different child to be photographed and captioned alongside its host family's activities. While for some parents it's a fun way to share their adventures, for others, it can strike a very real fear that their lack of outdoorsy pursuits will be exposed as Bernie Bear or Zoe Zebra spends a large part of the weekend face down on the carpet while they hunt panic-stricken for the remote control...

Ditch the Guilt!

Of course, being "outdoorsy" is a great thing to be but, similarly, there is no shame in being more "indoorsy"! Hiking up hills, walking in woods, foraging for fossils and suchlike, while very lovely things to do, don't necessarily equate to better parenting. A family can be just as happy and healthy being at home, snuggling on the sofa, enjoying a meal and – yes, despite the stigma – watching TV! It's no bad thing to get your child used to the idea that their free time doesn't have to be filled with constant activities. There is virtue in resting after a busy week at nursery. A safe, loving environment is an amazing thing to provide a child with and this is something to feel proud, not ashamed of.

THOU SHALT MAKE EVERYTHING BY HAND

Be it assembling a costume or baking cakes for a charity event, a mum's life can be littered with pressures for homespun makes. For many, it can be a persistent source of anxiety, and since research testifies it is mothers, not fathers, who are made to feel this burden, it really is a guilt-trip to bin.

DITCH THE GUILT!

If baking 30-odd non-allergenic brownies and glue-gunning glitter for various costume demands doesn't appeal, be it due to a lack of time or inclination, don't do it! There is no shame in your child taking store-bought cakes. Your skills may not lie in baking, but your child will know you have other talents. If it is time spent at work which stops you from baking, you are a role model to your child by proving you can make a success of being a working mother. However you fulfil the task, be it providing a costume or cakes, just do so without apology.

It's right to talk about motherhood as a wonderful thing, but we also need to talk about its stresses and strains.

———————————

CATHERINE,
PRINCESS OF WALES

THOU SHALT
NEVER BRIBE

"Do a pee-pee in your potty and Mummy will give you a chocolate button!" "Eat your greens and you can watch an hour of TV." "Tidy your room and we can go to soft play later." For many parents, these tactics are a means of helping a child associate applying effort and behaving well with positive consequences. Some, however, criticize such strategies for incentivizing a task, rather than encouraging a child to understand accountability for themselves and others. These are two schools of thought and neither is better than the other.

Ditch the Guilt!

Of course, chucking wads of cash at a child in exchange for good behaviour is probably not the best course of action – but that doesn't mean children rewarded with confectionery or gold stars for correctly using their potties are consequently going to grow into entitled, selfish adults! In fact, research shows that behaviours are more likely to happen again when followed by a positive consequence, such as a reward. This is called positive reinforcement and it has been proven to work extremely well with young children. If a reward chart or treat-based incentive feels right for you and your child, follow your gut – because quite simply, it's *your* call to make and not that of the "guilt police".

You always focus on your mistakes as a mum, and you just have to know that you're doing the best you can with what you know.

♥ VIOLA DAVIS

THOU SHALT BE THE SOURCE OF ALL KNOWLEDGE

Why is the sky blue? Why is water wet? Can dogs think in words? Is your head spinning yet? Helping a child understand the world can have you wondering if you need to complete an intensive Open University course in science in order to answer their myriad bizarre questions. It can also make you feel like you're failing your child when they're looking to you for knowledge you can't provide.

DITCH THE GUILT!

Firstly, you're not alone. Many parents will admit they struggle to deal with the barrage of questions. You can't possibly know everything and it is good for your child to realize that. You could research the topic together. Or, if you haven't got time, encourage your child to seek out the answer from another adult, a grandparent, or an older cousin, perhaps. That's no bad thing as you are teaching them to be resourceful. As they get older, their questions will get harder and they won't be able to rely on you all the time.

THOU SHALT BE A FUN PARENT

Singing *The Wheels on the Bus* on a loop and playing endless games of pat-a-cake can wear thin pretty quick – especially when it's eating into precious time for the mammoth to-do list that comes with parenting. Equally, hour-long homemade shows in the lounge, stories without end about how someone fell over in the playground and constant questions about why peas are green or cats can't fly, as any honest mum will tell you, can rapidly go from magical to monotonous motherhood moments.

Ditch the Guilt!

It's a rare parent who doesn't on occasion find themselves absent-mindedly scrolling through their phone at the playground or suppressing a big sigh at the prospect of yet another round of I Spy – and that's because, actually, sometimes, these things can be draining of both interest and time. Public service announcement: you're allowed to admit to this! And yes, there will be times when you'll feel like Mean Mummy for curtailing the fun in favour of toy tidying or even simply the need for a bit of peace. But it's all part and parcel of parenting and accepting that someone has to be in charge. Also, teaching your child that there are times when they have to make their own entertainment next to you because you need fifteen minutes to sit down with a hot drink or you have to tackle the to-do list is a valuable lesson. Research shows that solo play from a young age encourages children's creativity, develops their questioning mind and empowers them to problem solve without resorting to outside help all the time. Helping your child develop a curious mind by having a few minutes to yourself? That's nothing to feel guilty about!

THOU SHALT REMEMBER THE COMFORTER

There's a typical moment that most parents will recall with both horror and humour: the time they forgot, or worse, lost, their kid's favourite night-time toy. They'll perhaps shudder remembering how steps were anxiously retraced or how they desperately tried to recollect where they'd last seen it, as the dread of an unsettled night without it loomed large. It's a memory that, retrospectively, a parent might share with a wry smile. At the time, though, feeling responsible for the absence of the beloved comforter their child simply could not sleep without was less funny, rapidly escalating into a stressful situation that left them racked with remorse and self-irritation.

Ditch the Guilt!

Lots of parents who've experienced this will probably freely admit, at the time, they'd have happily sold a vital organ for the return of that night-time soother. But they'll also likely concede, nothing bad happened and while it was a tense moment and maybe did result in a fractious night, it's now remembered a little like a parenting milestone! Should you find yourself in such a situation, perhaps unpacking a bag for a trip away and realizing with panic that the crucial comforter is missing, think of this as a parenting rite of passage! It is without doubt that you will live to tell the lost-toy tale for the next generation of new parents certain to experience the same.

THOU SHALT BE ALL THINGS

No, thou shan't. Because mum burnout is a real thing and trying to be the outdoorsy, fun, wholesome, educating, perfect parent is a sure-fire way of finding out first-hand.

DITCH THE GUILT!

Write the following on a piece paper, tap it into a note on your phone, spell it out in fridge magnets or whatever else you prefer: "I can only do my best." Then commit this to memory, because your best is perfect.

I'm not a good mum;
I'm not a bad mum.
I'm the mum I am and
I try very hard, and
when I fail, that's OK.

———————

KRISTEN BELL

CASE STUDY

Toy Story

My husband James, myself and our two-year-old son Riad were on a family holiday for a week and I'd just unpacked Riad's case, when I got this creeping sense that something was missing. As I scanned his toys, I felt this surge of panic as I realized Riad's favourite stuffed monkey, Mimi, wasn't there. I remember shouting in dismay and James came running up the stairs of the holiday cottage. "I forgot Mimi!" I cried. James looked horrified for a moment and then, like he was in denial, said quietly: "Maybe she's just dropped somewhere?" He shot back downstairs and proceeded to search the entire car like it was a police raid! By the time James returned empty-handed, I'd remembered that I'd left Mimi by the front door, ironically as a reminder to myself to take her!

I'm not going to lie, Riad was in absolute bits at the prospect of a night without Mimi. I felt horrible; like I'd really let Riad down. I think I even shed a few of my own tears that night! And to be honest, Riad didn't go to bed easily at all, but, albeit with lots of resettling like he was a newborn again, he did finally sleep and that first night was the only really bad one of our week-long break.

Looking back, I could have been kinder to myself. It's such an easy mistake to make when you're dealing with a million and one things. But what I think is really indicative of the mum guilt I was feeling, was the way I blamed myself and said *I'd* forgot Mimi! As mothers, we often deal with so much that we hold ourselves accountable for everything child-related. In order to start shedding some of that unnecessary guilt, I really think mums need to shoulder far less.

SHENAZ, MUM OF TWO

BEING SOMEONE OTHER THAN "MUM"

Ever notice how fathers with jobs outside the home are rarely described as "working dads"? Have you observed too, that male celebrities who are also dads, are rarely quizzed in interviews about how they manage to juggle their careers with fatherhood? An identity outside of being a father is OK for dads and yet not for mothers, it would seem. Consequently, for many mums, the idea of indulging a sense of self away from motherhood can kickstart that demon guilt. For the sake of your well-being, not to mention the injustice of this, it's time to reject such outdated ideas and permit yourself to be someone other than Mum.

After giving birth there's a moment of rediscovery when you are making sure you still have goals and take care of yourself as a woman.

♥ BEYONCÉ

I AM HUMAN

The first, perhaps most-important, step in permitting yourself decent time to be someone other than "Mum", is acknowledging you have limits and mum burnout is a real thing. It's not easy to recognize burnout in yourself or in others, when everyone around you expects you to keep going and credits you with superpowers. Every new mum feels exhausted and overwhelmed at times, but if this is how you feel all the time and you find there is no space in your day to be "you" as well as "Mum" then you could be suffering from mum burnout. Acknowledging this doesn't mean you love your child less! Guilt does not serve as a useful emotion in any way in this context. Both mother and baby stand to gain if a mum embraces a life outside motherhood – and guilt will only ever undermine the advantages of this.

MUM'S GONE ON HOLIDAY

Psychologists frequently recommend that for new mums, taking time away is vital for avoiding burnout. But for prime rejuvenation, experts advise it should ideally be a break of at least two nights – and *without* the baby! For many this might not be feasible, but if it is viable in any way, taking a child-free trip can be a complete turning point when it comes to guilt. By doing something like this, completely for you – perhaps something that feels initially unthinkable and sends a surge of fear and shame coursing through you – you are grabbing guilt by the horns and slaying it.

Think of it a little like exposure therapy used for treating phobias; you're entering your worst-case scenario in order to help you gain control over those everyday, less intimidating, moments of guilt. Let's not forget why most people take a trip away in the first place – because they need a break! According to a travel survey, 77 per cent of its 2,000 participants described the need to break from their daily routines as their biggest reasons for booking a holiday. As a new mum, with a 24-7 daily grind to contend with, let's be frank, your needs are likely greater than average.

Almost everything
will work again if
you unplug it for
a few minutes,
including you.

———————————

ANNE LAMOTT

BABY'S BESTIE

As your baby grows, you might notice they seem particularly comfortable in the company of another baby – exploit this! Maybe you could suggest to your baby bestie's mum that you each take it in turns to give each other time out while the other watches the kids? Even just an hour could provide enough time to recharge and do something solely for yourself, perhaps get a haircut or go clothes shopping (no babywear purchases allowed!). Doing something like this as regularly as possible could do you the power of good and get you in the habit of focusing on yourself guilt-free. It's a win-win for both mums and babies – you're giving your little one the space to forge their very first friendship!

BACK-TO-WORK WORRIES

The prospect of returning to work after maternity leave can bring on a whole gamut of emotions for many new mothers and one of them, of course, is guilt. "How can I possibly hand my baby over for someone else to look after?" "What if I miss big milestones?" "What if I feel like I'm failing both at home and at work?" These are totally normal worries, but in truth, you will be fine, because if motherhood teaches you anything, your ability to cope and roll with the unexpected is pretty strong! Yes, there will likely be a period of adjustment and maybe, forgive the pun, a few teething problems, but both you and your baby will settle into a routine sooner than you know.

In fact, there are myriad reasons why bringing up a child as a working mum is beneficial to their upbringing. Recent research on men and women from 24 developed nations around the world found that women whose mothers worked throughout their childhood were more likely to have fulfilling careers themselves and men in the same position were more likely to take on a greater proportion of the household chores of their own families. Everyone benefits and there is certainly no room for guilt!

If you are worried about going back to work too abruptly, perhaps ask your employer about a phased return, to give you a chance to adjust. But most importantly, remember you're not failing your child by returning to paid work – you're providing for your child, and this is what a good parent does.

All I had to think about was myself. Now my children prevail. It doesn't mean my career is less important; I just have to position things differently.

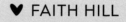 FAITH HILL

A DAILY DOSE
OF <u>YOU</u>

Sometimes life as a new mum can be so full-on, that it feels as if the most time you've taken for yourself in a day is a few very hurried toilet breaks! While this is totally understandable when life is so chaotic, try when possible to prevent this from becoming habitual. Consistently addressing your baby's needs but barely your own does not make for a sustainable healthy relationship with yourself. And of course, this sort of martyrdom is a very slippery road to guilt. Vow to do one thing, entirely for yourself, every day. Be it listening to a podcast or fixing yourself a nice lunch, just make sure it's a moment in your day all about you and your needs, and nothing at all to do with the baby.

REGULAR RECHARGE

A US survey of 2,000 mums found that the average mother spends 98 hours a week on parent-related tasks. That's roughly the equivalent of holding down two-and-a-half full-time jobs! So, we have Mother's Day – the one day of the year designated to celebrate mums? It's not enough, frankly. Motherhood, as that survey attests, is like no other job and such gruelling hours in another work environment would galvanize unions and HR departments into action! Taking time off to recharge shouldn't be seen as a luxury but rather a necessity – and often the people who need to recognize this most are mothers themselves.

Of course, for most, having a regular "day off" when you're a new mum is rarely feasible. However, as those nights become less disrupted (and if you're not there yet, don't lose heart, they *will*), make a weekly effort to spoil yourself in a deservedly indulgent manner. If possible, make it a recurring weeknight devoted to anything that takes your fancy – it could be a relaxing foot spa while reading a book, or a Thai takeaway followed by extravagant chocolates. Whatever you do, just acknowledge this as *your* evening of regular restoration, a preventive measure from burnout – and there should be no shame whatsoever associated with that.

I wasn't going to give up who I was before I had the baby. It's important to stay true to that as an example.

———————

CHRISTINA AGUILERA

Me-Time at Break Time

As many mums with jobs outside motherhood will admit, the daily lunch hour is one of the primary reasons to look forward to returning to work. It's unsurprisingly really, given that time enough to get dressed, let alone approximately 60 minutes to eat something, can be a real battle on maternity leave! While it's often tempting to turn a lunch break into chore-filled time – shopping for dinners, wipes, formula and whatever else is on that never-ending list of stuff to get – try to offset it with activities for yourself, too. Lunch with a colleague, a trip to the bookshop or even a manicure on occasion will help keep your mum-work balance in good health – and of course, allowing yourself to be a priority is a great guilt-minimizing practice!

DRESS YOUR OWN WAY!

As a time-poor new mum, your relationship with clothes may undoubtedly change. Perhaps that basic button-up top is whiffy after four consecutive days of wear, but it's also very convenient for breastfeeding. Possibly your collection of beautiful belts will give way to elasticated waistbands as comfort and ease take priority. And maybe a pair of trainers feel the safer bet over stylish but impractical kitten heels, for running around town with a baby in tow. There's nothing wrong, of course, with such shifts in your dress sense if it's necessity, not society, pressing you towards more practical wear...

Many mums report feeling the need to dress more for pragmatism than style, and consequently, opting for fashionable wardrobe choices can feel self-indulgent and even a bit shameful. What matters is that you're dressing for yourself, without worrying about what you should or shouldn't be wearing "as a mum". So, if you're in the mood for hitting the supermarket in head-to-toe fashion fit for a catwalk, fill your trendy boots *guilt-free!* Just be sure to live by your rules and not those dictated by some influencer or magazine.

Motherhood has a very humanizing effect. Everything gets reduced to essentials.

♥ MERYL STREEP

WILD IN THE AISLES

Perhaps pre-kids, a supermarket grocery shop was something of a chore – a bit like putting on a wash or cutting your toenails, a task you were keen to get over as quickly as possible. Maybe now a trip to the supermarket takes on a rosy nostalgic glow as you yearn for those carefree days when you could shop in peace without fear of a meltdown or the sudden need to locate facilities for an emergency baby change? Like many everyday things you possibly took for granted before becoming a mum, a weekly shop without a child, as many mothers will testify, practically feels like a spa break! So, if you get the opportunity to buy groceries alone, don't let guilt drive you to speed-shop. Take your time and savour that solitude in your supermarket of sanctuary.

BONDED FOR LIFE

Many mums, with a return to work looming on the horizon after maternity leave, worry about how the bond with their baby will be affected. Consequently, they also fear that the childcare provider will develop a closer relationship with their child than their own. It can be a strange dichotomy of feelings as on the one hand, you of course want a good support network for your baby, but on the other, there can be a creeping sense of threat and guilty resentment that you might somehow be replaced. It's totally natural to experience such emotions and this is nothing to be ashamed of. However, rest assured, your bond with your baby will not break. Yes, your baby is likely to form a close attachment to the caregiver in your absence, which is brilliant – but you will always mean the world to your little one, because your bond is second to none. Don't lose sight of this.

HOBBY LOBBY

If there was a particular pastime you enjoyed before becoming a mother, don't assume your relationship with it has to change. Admittedly, a lack of time and energy can be big factors for abandoning hobbies in the all-consuming early days of motherhood, but often, that pesky mum guilt is responsible for favourite pastimes biting the dust longer term. If lack of childcare is stopping you, you may still be able to pursue your hobbies with baby in tow. If running is your thing, why not run with the pram? If you miss your pre-baby yoga class, see if there is an online class you could attend. Singing, cooking, painting, birdwatching, axe-throwing – whatever the hobby, refuse to let guilt rob you of the things you enjoy doing.

MADE-UP MUM

In much the same way some mums feel a personal and societal pressure to dress down when they become parents, many also feel, particularly as a new mother, a pressure to swerve the make-up. Sometimes you feel there just isn't time or it's too much effort. If you enjoyed wearing make-up before motherhood and want to continue doing so, this is entirely your choice. It's not the concern of anyone else and you certainly shouldn't feel shamed for choosing to do so! Equally, if you prefer not to wear make-up, this again is no one else's business. All that matters is that it's not a sense of guilt around social expectations that's dictating your choices and keeping your identity wholly as "Mum".

SWEET SEROTONIN

Research has revealed that mothers who document a happy moment at the end of each day to reflect on will sleep better, feel more self-confident and boost their levels of that all-important happiness hormone, serotonin. Reflection is great for positively boosting a frame of mind, and also, a very useful tool for maintaining a sense of self on the days when motherhood feels overwhelming. Try it! So, instead of dwelling on the baby-related challenges of your day, focus on what you managed to achieve for yourself. Perhaps keep a happy moment diary by your bed. Even if all you note is drinking a whole cup of tea while it was still hot, or watching an episode of your favourite TV show, these small wins are important. They are signs to yourself that you're recognizing you have needs, and that you matter.

FUTURE GOALS

A great exercise for keeping a healthy sense of self is compiling a list of things you'd like to achieve for yourself in the future. It could be anything from learning a new language to writing a book – ideally nothing too pressured. Just jot down a set of goals that feel exciting and inspiring when you think about them. Keep that list somewhere handy and revisit it, adding to it if you wish, particularly on those days when motherhood feels relentless.

You need much
more sensitivity in
the workplace to
the challenges young
women go through in
trying to do two very
difficult jobs well.

_____

HILLARY CLINTON

CHANGE THE SUBJECT!

It's natural to talk about motherhood a lot when you first become a mum; and it's understandable, particularly with another new mother, when it's the go-to topic of conversation. However, if you're feeling bored solely exchanging baby-related chat – and find yourself switching off hearing about the minutiae of nappy changes, sleeping habits and night-time feeds – don't be afraid to change the subject! Be as subtle or direct as suits, but don't feel obliged to pursue a dialogue that you feel stifled by.

GET OUT!

Studies reveal in order to feel the chemical benefits of human interaction, including serotonin and the bonding hormone oxytocin, we should ideally socialize with our friends twice a week. As a new mum, of course, this sort of frequency might sound as likely as a newborn sleeping soundly for a 12-hour stretch – and let's be honest, often your bed is far more appealing than a busy bar. However, in terms of being someone other than "Mum", it can be just the tonic you need. Try and catch up with the pals you love most and do it with whatever sort of regularity you can manage because the more you do this, the better you'll get at managing any potential guilt. Dinner, dancing, concerts, comedy nights – whatever your preference, just make it frequent, in the company of your closest friends, and complete and utter fun.

ESTABLISHING WORK BOUNDARIES

According to a UK survey, two in five mothers with jobs outside of motherhood say they feel judged by their colleagues and seniors for finishing on time and have even felt held back from getting a promotion because of it. With many jobs now structured as hybrid or fully from home, drawing a line in the sand between a job and family life can be even trickier. However, establishing boundaries, whatever your working arrangement, is crucial, particularly as a means of minimizing misplaced guilt.

If you're returning to work after maternity leave, from the outset let people know what time you'll be finishing each day. You can be polite and clear – but don't feel or express an apologetic sense of shame around this. You have *nothing* to feel guilty for – and leaving on time doesn't make you any less productive or effective. In order for you to truly enjoy your return to work and your time away from motherhood duties, it's important for everyone, including yourself, to accept and accommodate this part of your identity.

I can start doing all the things I used to do without feeling too much of that mother's guilt. It's a good place to be at.

♥ FEARNE COTTON

CASE STUDY

My Solo Weekend

When my partner Claire suggested I take a break by myself, without her or the baby, I thought she was joking. I was feeling low and I think we were both concerned I might be experiencing some postnatal depression. Our daughter Rosie was seven months at the time and while things were actually a lot better with regards to sleep and some routine – everything had been so tough going previously, particularly with colic – things had caught up with me and I was feeling depleted. Claire was so supportive, and during a heart-to-heart after I'd had a particularly bad day at home with Rosie, she suddenly asked me: "What would make you happy?"

"A spa break alone!" I joked.

"So let's book you one!" she replied, and when I realized she was serious, I was trying to get out of it because the prospect scared me so much!

But I did go on the spa break alone – and for a whole weekend! And honestly, it was total bliss. I had a massage, read a book, ate a two-course meal and watched a movie in my room, and the best bit of course – I slept! Getting away not only improved my mental health, but it was also such a huge turning point for Claire and me. That weekend was the first she'd experienced caring for Rosie alone and she admitted that she then fully understood the intensity of looking after a child at a home. But the thing I learned most from that weekend away was that it's not just OK to allow yourself space – it's actually crucial.

OVERCOMING
MUM GUILT

For this final chapter, overcoming mum guilt is broken down into tips for robust mental health and ways in which to adopt a different frame of mind. Some ideas may suit your personality, while others less so. What's important is that you invest time and effort when you can to address guilt in order to manage it – because misplaced guilt does not deserve your precious energy.

I've had to learn
to release myself from
mum guilt at least a
couple times a day.

———————

MINDY KALING

Baby Love

Gazing intently at you, wiggling and kicking their legs at the sound of your voice, and of course, the heart-melting way your baby's face lights up and breaks into a gorgeous gummy smile at the sight of your face – these are all indicators of just how much of a bond your baby has with you. Preserve each and every moment in your memory, because these are the ways in which your baby is reflecting right back the unconditional love you give. Let this love reassure you; you have absolutely nothing to feel guilty for.

APPLY YOUR MASK FIRST!

Most people are familiar with the safety advice flight attendants give on planes: "It's important to apply your own oxygen mask before assisting others, particularly young children." And while it might be a familiar analogy often applied to self-care, there is a lot of sense to take from this idiom as a mum. Far too often, mums express feeling guilty about prioritizing themselves over their children, but how can you be of help to anyone without sufficient strength to do so? Whether you need to eat, bathe or pee before dealing with your child, remind yourself, you're meeting your needs in order to efficiently meet theirs.

MOTHER LOVE

Neuroscience findings suggest the reason a toddler is often very excited to explore the world around them is because they feel secure enough to do so. Essentially, they have established so much trust in the security and nurture provided for them as babies, they feel ready for adventure! Remember this, firstly, when you're chasing after your toddler who's decided it will be great fun to bolt from you in the supermarket, and, secondly, whenever doubts about your abilities as a mother are gnawing at you. Never underestimate how much you've done and continue to do for your child.

My mother
was my role
model before
I even knew
what that was.

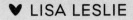 LISA LESLIE

DAWN MEANDER

Many mums with early rising or sleep-reluctant children will be familiar with rude dawn awakenings. While the temptation might be to sleepily shuffle to the kitchen for a massive mug of coffee and slump in front of morning TV, you might be surprised to hear that you will benefit more from heading out for a walk within the first hour of waking up. Dawn daylight has been proven to effectively clear the sleep hormone melatonin, known for its slumberous qualities, out of the bloodstream, lending your brain the clarity it needs to focus and feel more positive. This is especially helpful for keeping negative thinking, and the mum guilt this so often brings, at bay.

TRIM THE TO-DO LIST

If you have a "to-do" list, be it on your phone or on a piece of paper, take a look at it. Does this list feel like a source of pressure, and thus create guilt you could do without? If so, ask yourself a few questions. Could any of this load be shared? Is there anything you could put off entirely until life is a little less busy? Are some of these tasks really necessary? Try to be firm with yourself. Yes, a birthday text might feel less special than a card, but a good friend will understand that life is pretty chaotic right now. Fair enough, it's easier to see all the special offers when you are in the supermarket, but an online delivery could be a brilliant means of conserving precious time and energy. Once you start whittling, you might soon realize there's less on that list that's urgent or necessary than you thought.

Other Mother Knows Best

Perhaps there's another mum in your circle of friends or neighbourhood, who makes motherhood look like a breeze. Perhaps you've enviously observed an energetic, carefree demeanour that doesn't resemble your own in any way, shape or form and listened to tales of restful nights and struggle-free routines, that again, couldn't be further from your experience. But perhaps, unbeknownst to you and just like you, that mum is contending with similar insecurities and self-reproach. Try to resist judging yourself unfavourably to other mothers because often those comparative feelings of inadequacy are based on nothing more than speculation. Most crucially, this sort of unhelpful comparison accentuates a sense of guilt that is completely unfounded.

Whether
stay-at-home
or working, finding
that balance with
kids is a true art.
I'm here to say:
if you are having a
rough day or week –
it's OK – I am, too!

———————

SERENA WILLIAMS

BIG BOOK OF HOW-TO BABY

Often, a new mother will find the bedside table suddenly sprouting, either gifted or bought, a big pile of baby books. Some of the advice these books offer can be really helpful. Others, however, can be detrimental, particularly with regard to heightening mum guilt. "By seven months, babies typically sleep 11 hours a night." "Baby should start talking around 18 months." "A child not potty-trained by the age of two may continue to have accidents for the next three years." Such statements are generalizations and don't take into account that a child's development is unique and particularly, as most parents will tell you, there is no such thing as "typical" when it comes to a baby's routine. So, take a look at those titles claiming to offer baby-related tips and tricks – are any of them feeling less like a useful resource and more a source of pressure? If so, bin that big pile of how-to baby books now!

SEEDS OF CHANGE

According to research, surrounding yourself with indoor plants works wonders for well-being. Plants can increase concentration by as much as 20 per cent, speed up recovery from illness, help with memory retention and freshen the air by removing pollutants and absorbing them into their leaves and roots. It might feel like an arbitrary means of overcoming mum guilt, but you may want to consider investing in plants around your home to encourage a more positive frame of mind. Quick tip, though: perhaps go for low-maintenance plants like cacti and dragon trees. You want plants to enhance your energy levels, not drain them!

MUM MIRTH

The online mum world is not without fault. But amid the #gifted posts, smug selfies and tips from the parenting police is a hub of "honest parenting" accounts sharing their bad days, turning "failures" into reasons to smile and laugh. This sort of camaraderie is a brilliant collective way of finding the funny in challenging and often potentially guilt-laden situations. Wishing you were anywhere but at home during Witching Hour? You're not alone! Forgot your appointment at the baby clinic? Who hasn't! A coffee shop meet-up cut short by a sudden poonami and no spare clothes? Laugh! Because these "parenting fails" aren't fails at all – just the everyday life of a pretty typical mum.

Don't be hard on yourself... It's worth it to recharge once a week: get sleep, have a date night or a girls' night in, and drink some wine!

♥ JESSICA ALBA

CUP OF ME

When guilt feels overwhelming, sometimes just sitting down with a hot drink and being mindful in that moment of respite can do wonders for well-being. Japanese research has proven that fully committing and "ritualizing" your time for a break can allow for a more relaxed, reflective headspace. At the quietest point of your day – perhaps while your baby's napping or sitting happily in a bouncer – create your own routine by slowing down the whole process of making yourself a drink. If it is tea, use a teapot and a cup and saucer, perhaps. Maybe listen to your favourite playlist or light a candle as you sip. Design your ritual to feel like a pause in your day where you focus solely on yourself.

TALKING SCENT

A quick-and-easy mindful method to help quieten thoughts of worry and guilt is achieved simply by lighting a candle. Perhaps you don't think that burning candles is for you, but there is much scientific evidence to support this as a great source of mindfulness. The flickering flame is proven to reduce stress and can even help you to achieve a more meditative frame of mind, as your brain associates the low light with relaxation. As you feel more tranquil, you will also fall asleep more easily, strengthen your immune system and improve your overall emotional state.

Studies have also shown that candles with a soothing scent like lavender or camomile can further decrease levels of cortisol, too. Scientists in the field of cognitive neuroscience have proven that the human sense of smell affects 75 per cent of our daily emotions and is very strongly connected with memory as well as well-being. Perhaps try a scented candle after your baby's bath and bedtime. While carefully observing the candle and appreciating the scent, take note of how both your mind and body feel afterwards. You might need to try a few different fragrance varieties to suit, but once you find your fit, the potential stress-relieving benefits can be amazing. You are also creating through the sense of smell a memory for you and your baby of these early days.

Learning my own boundaries while trying to take care of my son was hard. But I had a great support system.

———————

BRENDA SONG

Think Positive

When you're in the eye of a particularly difficult phase of parenting, it's easy to become so preoccupied with your current situation that you feel like you're living in a state of misery without end. Neuroscientists have discovered that by simply allowing your brain to think positively of the future, your current circumstances can feel less relentless and infinite as calming neurotransmitters are released in the brain. When new parenting life is feeling hard to bear, write a list of everything you're looking forward to doing with your child, beyond the existing challenges. Keep it handy and consistently add to it if you can. You can revisit this list whenever your parenting perspective needs a positive lens.

It's all overwhelming because your brain knows you need to be at work and your heart wants to be with your kids... I think it's important to do both.

♥ RACHEL ZOE

PRAISE YOU

In order to minimize potential detrimental guilt, particularly as a new mum, you need to make a concerted effort to regularly talk kindly to yourself. Try it now. Look at what specifically makes you feel guilty and then address those issues as a sympathetic best friend or loving family member might. What would this person say to support and reassure you? What kind words would they use? Now, tell them to yourself, with conviction. Do it as an inner monologue, vocalized or written down – whatever suits. Just make sure you devote sufficient, habitual time, preferably on a daily basis, to reminding yourself that, actually, regardless of what the day has entailed, you rock and your baby is lucky to have you.

If you are experiencing mum guilt, take a deep breath and allow it.

MARISSA JOHNSON

THE MEDITATION GAME

Meditation has been proven to be an effective means of "resetting" your way of thinking when negative, self-critical thoughts start creeping in. Try this mindful meditation routine that can be practised anywhere.

Choose a natural object from within your immediate environment and focus on it. Look at this object as if you're seeing it for the first time. Visually explore every aspect of it for as long as your concentration can manage. Finish by closing your eyes, inhaling deeply to the count of five and then exhaling slowly as you open your eyes.

Meditation can take a while to master, but with regular practice – particularly when your frame of mind needs a reboot – it can be a game changer.

POONAMI!

Many parents and carers will be familiar with the word "poonami". It's a term in which a baby very suddenly has an explosive bowel evacuation. It's messy and rarely fun to deal with, but generally not a sign of anything serious. Many will also know there's very little you can do to prevent a poonami from striking, as it so often does, when you're out and about, far from home. Preparing for it with things like spare clothes and extra wipes is as much as you can do. This a good metaphor for approaching parental guilt – because let's face it, to borrow (less frankly) from another well-known phrase, sh*t happens!

It's not about stoically resigning yourself to bad things occurring. It's about recognizing that your efforts are better invested in what you can influence. There will always be events and circumstances in life you feel powerless over, especially as a new parent, but fixating on these with worry or guilt isn't helpful. Try to look at these unfortunate situations with a positive mindset. Positive thinking doesn't mean you should ignore life's unpleasant events; it simply equips you to cope better with them, laugh about them and notice the positive aspects of the day. Accepting things beyond your control helps you think rationally, have faith in your abilities to cope and, ultimately, move on.

Make sure you have people around you that can give you support and help, whether it's best friends, family members, or a babysitter.

♥ DEBRA MESSING

TUB TIME

Having a bath is self-care with scientifically proven benefits. A warm bath can help improve your blood flow, lift low moods, alleviate muscle pain, help you sleep better and kill bacteria, thus reducing the risk of catching nasty bugs. So, while it might feel a little decadent to have a bath, especially when life is so busy with a baby, think of it as devoting time specifically for your mental and physical well-being – and also as a good exercise in the fight against guilt! Tell yourself as you enjoy your bath, this isn't decadence – it's essential maintenance you deserve.

WRITE IN THE HEAD

Psychological studies have confirmed that there is a relationship between journaling, mental catharsis and increased self-awareness, with many notable fans using it as a well-being tool, from Albert Einstein and Nelson Mandela to Jennifer Aniston and Oprah Winfrey. For many, it can provide a therapeutic source of managing stress, dumping worries and practising gratitude. It can also prove an effective method of overcoming guilt when things feel overbearing.

You don't have to keep a daily journal to feel the benefits of this. It could be once a week or whenever you feel the need to write. Try adopting some writing prompts to help you regularly focus specifically on countering any self-criticism which so often leads to guilt. You could ask yourself: *What positive parenting qualities make me unique?* You could list: *Three things I'm most proud of achieving today.* You might complete the following sentence: *My baby is lucky to have me for a mum, because...* Don't put pressure on yourself to do it when exhaustion is sapping you of momentum; just write when energy levels permit. Also, don't be modest. Nobody else is going to read your notes. Positive self-talk is not about vanity – it's about emotional regulation and ditching guilt for a more productive frame of mind.

Now that my kids are older, I think it's pretty badass and cool for them to see their mum do what she loves to do.

———————

TAMERA MOWRY

REACH OUT

If you feel that guilt is leading to severe anxiety or any form of mental health issue overwhelming your life, this should be addressed professionally. There are huge benefits to be gained from talking to someone, so make that first step by reaching out to your doctor, a trained counsellor or a reputable local support group. Try not to be deterred if a course of action doesn't sit comfortably with or work for you – something else might, so keep trying. What's important is that you don't ignore your needs. You, and your baby, deserve better than that.

Expect the Unexpected

There is a saying: expectation is the root of all heartache. This is never truer than of parenting. As the well-known book title goes: what to expect when you're expecting? The unexpected! There will be days when that evening's dinner is whatever can be quickly concocted from the cupboard because a planned supermarket trip had to be abandoned for a late nap. There will be appointments, baby groups and commutes to work where you're running so late there's barely time to brush your teeth. There will be times when your baby might fuss and cling to you so much that the day entails little beyond cuddling and placating your little one. The best course of action? Let it go! Allow yourself to feel a little frustrated of course, but never remorseful about what you haven't been able to achieve or control.

DON'T FORGET YOU!

While motherhood is without a doubt something to be enormously proud of, solely defining yourself as a mum can mean you lose sight of who you are outside motherhood and consequently, your identity starts to feel like an appendage. This mindset is instrumental in contributing to maternal guilt, because the message you're sending yourself is that you matter less. Work at changing this mindset! Start by greeting people with your name first and not your child's, particularly in any sort of baby group setting where this is often the case. No more: "Hi, I'm Jack's mum," or "This is Amina! She's six months..." Say your name loud and proud! It doesn't mean you love your baby less.

It's great when the kids know that both Mummy and Daddy work, and that we're equal.

♥ VICTORIA BECKHAM

CASE STUDY

Self-Compassion Is Key

When I had my eldest, now 11, my family and friends use to joke about how often I'd start sentences, when I was talking about something motherhood-related, with: "I feel bad because..." "I feel bad because I have to work late and my in-laws have to pick up my daughter from nursery," or "I feel bad because I'm replying to emails on my phone when I'm supposed to be playing a game." It was a friend who pointed out that this catchphrase I'd adopted since becoming a mum was not helpful. She made me realize that I was putting myself down and that was a shame, because it was blighting my joy of motherhood.

CASE STUDY

I've had two more since my first – one is seven and the other just three – and it's taken a lot of time and effort, but I think I'm now much better at being kind to myself when I start to feel guilt getting the better of me. I really make an effort to not talk negatively about myself, either to other people or internally. But most importantly, and this was something my friend also said which made me cry, I know I'm a loving mum doing my best and ultimately, this is absolutely all that matters.

BECKY, MUM OF THREE

Am I getting it right?
Not all the time.
Mama guilt?
Obviously... I know
this is a process.

_____

HILARIA BALDWIN

FINAL THOUGHTS

Conquering mum guilt is no easy feat, especially given society's perception that, when it comes to child-rearing, a mother should bear all responsibility. However, as frustrating as that is, what helps in the battle against guilt is recognizing that this form of social pressure is asking for the unfeasible, and as this book has explored throughout, you need to cut yourself some serious slack – especially when the odds are stacked so unfairly against you.

Throughout motherhood, you will inevitably experience guilt in some way or another – you are an amazing mum so it's only natural – but that guilt should in no way dictate what your life looks like and how you bring up your child. Whenever guilt does strike more often than you feel comfortable with, flick through these pages and remind yourself of the following:

- You don't have supernatural powers.

- You can't be in two places at once.

- You can't time travel and change the course of an action.

- You don't thrive on turbo energy.

- You can't exist without sleep.

- You don't have the ability to achieve the impossible.

Just like your baby, you are human, made of flesh and blood, and you too are experiencing a new life. However, a lack of unearthly powers aside, one thing is certain: to your baby, you are definitely a superhero.

RESOURCES

BOOKS

Hayes, Ann and Andrew, Rachel *The Supermum Myth* (2017, White Ladder Press)

Mathur, Anna *Mind Over Mother* (2020, Piatkus)

Smith, Julie *Why Has Nobody Told Me This Before?* (2022, Michael Joseph)

Sims, Gill *Why Mummy Drinks* (2018, HarperCollins) – there are more books in the series

PODCASTS

The Motherkind Podcast: www.motherkind.co/podcast Experts discussing everything from how to calm a toddler to dealing with anxiety.

The Scummy Mummies Podcast: www.scummymummies.com/blogs/podcast A comedy podcast for less-than-perfect parents.

Mommy's on a Call: www.stephanieuchima.com/podcast Mothers in business talk about parenting, holistic health, wellness and mindfulness.

Not Another Mummy Podcast:
shows.acast.com/notanothermummy
Interviews and advice on parenting and family issues.

Rose and Rosie Parental Guidance:
open.spotify.com/show/667zSZZjcHnm2cs5KWyyZ3
A comedian couple adventure into
parenthood and beyond.

Motherhood in Black and White:
blackandwhitemomcast.buzzsprout.com
Two women from different worlds come together
to share experiences of motherhood.

WEBSITES AND HELPLINES

Mumsnet: www.mumsnet.com
A vast community and resource full of knowledge,
advice and support on everything from
conception, childbirth, babies and teenagers
to physical and mental health worries.

Mind: www.mind.org.uk / 0300 123 3393
Support and tips for living with a variety
of mental health conditions.

Mental Health America: www.mhanational.org
Practical advice and support, including links to online
communities and tools for long-term wellness.

Crisis Text Line:
US: Text HOME to 741741 to connect
with a trained crisis counsellor.
UK: Text SHOUT to 85258 to text with
a trained crisis volunteer.
Ireland: Text HOME to 50808.
A 24/7 mental health text service in the
US, Canada, UK and Ireland.

Samaritans (UK and Ireland):
www.samaritans.org / 116 123
Emotional support for anyone in distress,
struggling to cope or at risk of suicide.

**Samaritans (US): www.samaritansusa.org /
1 (800) 273-TALK**
Suicide prevention centres in the US.

SANE (AUS) – www.sane.org / 1800 187 263
Information and crisis support for people with
mental health challenges and their families.

Mother Power

**A Feminist's Guide
to Motherhood**

ISBN: 978-1-80007-278-7

Know and grow your mother power!

The journey of motherhood is a physical and emotional roller coaster, and there's often little or no time to stop and consider your own needs, at least not without feeling guilty about it. This is where *Mother Power* comes in – a reassuring parenting guide that's always in your corner.

This wake-up call for mums everywhere will demonstrate how looking after your own well-being can make you a better parent. Fully embrace motherhood, find your flow and unlock your greatness.

Have you enjoyed this book?
If so, why not write a review
on your favourite website?

If you're interested in finding out more
about our books, find us on Facebook at
Summersdale Publishers, on Twitter at
@Summersdale and on Instagram and
TikTok at **@summersdalebooks** and get
in touch. We'd love to hear from you!

Thanks very much for buying
this Summersdale book.

www.summersdale.com